Penny Stocks

Making Money with The Ultimate Quick Start Guide for Beginners

Andrew C. Ellis

The follow eBook is reproduced below with the goal of providing information that is as accurate and reliable as possible. Regardless, purchasing this eBook can be seen as consent to the fact that both the publisher and the author of this book are in no way experts on the topics discussed within and that any recommendations or suggestions that are made herein are for entertainment purposes only. Professionals should be consulted as needed prior to undertaking any of the action endorsed herein.

This declaration is deemed fair and valid by both the American Bar Association and the Committee of Publishers Association and is legally binding throughout the United States.

Furthermore, the transmission, duplication or reproduction of any of the following work including specific information will be considered an illegal act irrespective of if it is done electronically or in print. This extends to creating a secondary or tertiary copy of the work or a recorded copy and is only allowed with express written consent from the Publisher. All additional right reserved.

The information in the following pages is broadly considered to be a truthful and accurate account of facts and as such any inattention, use or misuse of the information in question by the reader will render any resulting actions solely under their purview. There are no scenarios in which the publisher or the original author of this work can be in any fashion deemed liable for any hardship or damages that may befall them after undertaking information described herein.

Additionally, the information in the following pages is intended only for informational purposes and should thus be thought of as universal. As befitting its nature, it is presented without assurance regarding its prolonged validity or interim quality. Trademarks that are mentioned are done without written consent and can in no way be considered an endorsement from the trademark holder.

Table of Contents

Introduction

Congratulations on downloading *Penny Stocks: The Ultimate Quick Start Guide for Beginners* and thank you for doing so.

The following chapters will discuss quite a lot of things about penny stocks. At this point, you probably already know a rudimentary amount about penny stocks - after all, they're pretty much everywhere. You hear about them all the time from family or friends who are new to investing and trying to find their way, as well as on television and in pretty much any discussion about penny stocks.

Penny stocks can be a dangerous game to invest in. Cheap does not always necessitate good, and the fact that penny stocks are cheap and their companies relatively unestablished means that they're certainly not as much of a safe investment as an investment in a more sound and safe company.

However, with that said, penny stocks are unique and interesting in and of themselves, and there's a lot for somebody to know about them. They're an extremely rewarding investing concept to learn about and some people have even gotten rich off of penny stock trading.

This book is going to cover quite a bit. Over the course of this book, we're going to be talking about what exactly penny stocks are, the pros and cons for investing in penny stocks, the risk behind penny stocks and how to manage that risk, where to look for penny stocks and a broker, choosing which stock to trade, and trading essentials like share price and valuation, the three best trading strategies for new traders, and the most common traps that a lot of new traders will fall into.

Over the course of this book, you're going to be learning a lot - a whole lot. The pace may seem a little bit fast at times, but I assure you that if you stick with it to the end and allow me to teach you all about this volatile type of security, you'll have a firm grasp on the trading and market mechanisms of one of the most high-risk high-reward means of securities trading out there. The fact that it also happens to be the most fun one is simply a bonus.

There are plenty of books on this subject on the market, so thanks again for choosing this one! Every effort was made to ensure it is full of as much useful information as possible, please enjoy!

Chapter 1: What are Penny Stocks? Why are They Good/Bad?

Penny stocks are a relatively simple thing in principle. In other countries, they're commonly known as "cent stocks". In both names, they represent the same thing: a stock which has a low price (often less than a dollar) with a small market cap (under $500 million).

These stocks are usually traded off of the generally used market exchanges. For example, you'll hardly ever find a penny stock on NASDAQ or the New York Stock Exchange.

So what purpose do they serve? Well, several, but the largest is that they help a company procure capital in order to become larger and, consequently, more powerful. Through the market, they're able to build up the money that they need in order to make a strong investment

Penny stocks generally are traded to the benefit of a smaller public company. The stocks become offered on a marketplace just like any other stock out there: through an initial public offering. This process is three-fold.

Step one for a company looking to be publicly traded is for them to either:

- complete a statement of registration for the SEC, or
- state why their public offering would be exempt from the process of registration in the first place

They also must make certain to check the laws regarding securities trading relevant to the states in which they're looking to sell the stock.

Step two, after the SEC's approval of the registration

statement, is that the company starts the process of getting stock orders from enterprising traders.

Step three, once all of that is done, is that the company applies to have the stock traded listed on an exchange, such as the aforementioned NASDAQ and New York Stock Exchange. It can also be sold on over-the-counter marketplaces such as the OTC Bulletin Board or the OTC Markets Group (also commonly referred to as Pink Sheets).

Penny stocks are almost always sold on over-the-counter exchanges. This is majorly because larger exchanges tend to have incredibly stringent policies towards what is allowed to trade on them and what companies can list what sorts of stocks. Most penny stocks come nowhere near meeting the requirements of these larger exchanges, and what's more is that getting listed on these exchanges costs a *lot* of money and comes with a lot of stringent regulation, both of which can be quite heavy on a blossoming company's already (relatively) small supply of funding.

With all this in mind, penny stocks turn out to be a pretty great deal for smaller companies, at least in a comparative sense. They allow the company to build up quite a lot of capital in a relatively easy way, and let the company get a very firm hold on whatever market they're in by the large amounts of investitures.

So now that we actually know a thing or two about penny stocks, how about we establish what makes them a good (and a bad) idea?

First off, let me be clear. Penny stocks are a bad idea in a *lot* of ways. This doesn't mean you should be discouraged from learning about penny stock training, not at all. Rather, I'm just trying to be a bit honest because money is money, and money is thus important.

It's important to remember that there is risk involved.

However, if you bear that in mind and educate yourself before you make any big move toward penny stocks, you may just have what it takes to not make any major mistakes. This is just a forewarning because penny stocks are known well for their volatility and speculative nature, which could catch an unknowing (or unready) investor off-guard.

Again, this is not to discourage you. In fact, penny stocks are a fun and fulfilling trading means for a great number of reasons.

Pros

The biggest factor which makes penny stocks a lot of fun to work with is the fact that penny stocks are, by their very nature, the next big companies in the future. A huge number of companies out there are just starting out and are turning to penny stocks as a means to raise capital in order to build themselves.

This is a deciding factor in what makes a lot of people work with penny stocks. The idea of being on the forefront of the world at large and being a contributor to the next Apple or Google can be (and is!) a major driver for a lot of people who decide that they'd like to invest in penny stocks. Think about how cool it would be to look back in 10 years and know that you made a mark on the world by investing in a company that is absolutely huge now!

This brings us to the next major point for which people enjoy working with and investing in penny stocks: the fact that they can turn a small amount of money into veritable stacks of cash. How does this happen? Well, we've already established that penny stocks are very cheap and the shares are incredibly cost efficient. Shares are incredibly cheap and the money which you invest goes much further. For example, if you have 250 dollars to invest and are able to buy 500 shares of a company, and then those shares shoot up to about $10 each after the company in which you invested sees a majorly successful product launch or something similar, then your initial 250 dollars is now worth about 50,000 dollars. That's a lot of money to make off of next to nothing.

This, of course, brings us to the next part: penny stocks are *exciting*. They're an absolute blast to work with. When you think of the financial sector and the game of trading stocks and options and so forth, "exhilarating" is most likely not one of the first words that comes to mind. However, penny stock trading can, to an extent, be an exhilarating experience. The fact is that it feels really, really great to see your money become something from next to nothing, and every positive shift in those initial shares that you bought will make you absolutely awash in delight. Penny stocks aren't passive. They require your full attention, but you won't even be complaining about that because you'll be so enthralled in the process.

Which brings us to the last point: part of what makes penny stocks so attractive and exhilarating is the fact that they move *fast*. There are no breaks on the penny stock train, period. Because of the nature of penny stock and exchanges thereof, penny stocks usually don't see gradual shifts. Rather, you'll see a massive increase in price at one time.

However, this is where the bad comes in. You need to be aware and cautious that you aren't necessarily going to have a great experience with penny stocks at all. There are many reasons which may make penny stocks a poor investment choice.

Cons

The first major hang-up that should probably cause a double take before you get into penny stock investing is the fact that a lot of the companies simply aren't *good*. There's a reason that a lot of them are on the penny stock exchange. Granted, some of them are newer, but that doesn't mean they automatically have a strong team behind them, either. For a lot of penny stock companies, they can very easily find themselves mismanaged and being dragged down by an altogether horrible set of circumstances. Maybe they aren't drawing a profit and they're in economic catastrophe. Maybe their product simply *isn't* good, or their industry is too competitive or nearly dead. One way or another, a lot of companies on the penny stock exchange simply aren't good.

Not only are the companies not good,, but often, the marketplaces are unreliable as well. They often have few, or no, regulations to ensure the quality of both the transactions and the companies on them. This doesn't make them untrustworthy, necessarily - you just shouldn't expect them to be anything like the American Stock Exchange or something of the like because, plainly, it won't be. They are nothing alike. The marketplaces for penny stocks are used by less reputable companies for a reason, and that's because the marketplaces are of a far lower caliber than others.

The combination of the above two factors contributes to yet another. Most people who invest in penny stocks will end up losing money. Penny stocks are incredibly speculative by their very nature and you won't be treated well to trust on them as a source of income. The vast majority of penny stock transactions don't go favorably.

There's no clever segue for this but you should also consider that penny stocks are incredibly illiquid. "Illiquid" and "liquidity" in general refer to a commodity or stock's ability to be bought and sold without a major shift in price. More accurately, it's the likelihood that the person who buys something directly after somebody sells it will be buying it at the same rate at which the other person sold it. This is an ugly explanation, I know, but it's a rather difficult concept to explain. This means essentially that a stock is sold often and its price moves smoothly and naturally as a response to the constant selling and buying of the stock in question.

The lack of this feature of "liquidity" means that these stocks have yet another quality: the fact that they are massively volatile. I actually mentioned this as a pro. And it is a pro! When your cards are right, at least. When they aren't, however, this means essentially that you're not going to be very well off in the end. Nobody wants the cards stacked against them, and when prices can rise and tank in a matter of days making an investment either a soaring success or an absolute failure, it's not exactly becoming of the whole penny stock market that it could so easily ruin everything.

All of this leads up to the last consideration: there are a *lot* of pump and dumps and scams which take place on the penny stock marketplace. There are a lot of reasons for this and there are equally as many ways that these may manifest. These generally take place by somebody building up a fake hype for a penny stock by claiming that they have insider information or something of the like. They make their investment prior, of course, and then everybody starts to buy the penny stock. The person (or organization - organizations, too, will take part in this sort of scam) then sells their now massively profitable stocks before anybody else is any the wiser as to the actual value of the penny stock (that is to say, none at all).

This, of course, doesn't bode well for penny stock hopefuls because it means it's very easy to get caught up in various traps and misread a lot of market movement in an already volatile stock trading environment.

That actually reminds me of another thing which may cause you some trouble down the road. Everything that happens on the penny stock market is moving much faster than things which happen on more established trading markets. By the very nature of penny stock marketplaces, they tend to not have terribly historied stocks. What does this mean for you as a wishful investor? Well, it means that you don't have much of a history to *go off of*. This isn't good for you. A stock's history is incredibly important in knowing how stable it is, how it has performed historically, and generally whether or not it's a good investment in the first place.

The important thing to remember about penny stocks is that when you use them, you are gambling in a way.

There are, of course, a lot of risks to penny stocks. There are, likewise, a lot of possible payoffs. But they're unpredictable, incredibly volatile, and it's very difficult to know exactly the path that a company is going to take. In fact, I'm going to argue that it's impossible to know *exactly* what path something is going to take anyway, and the nature of the entire affair only makes it more difficult for you to tell how a stock is going to go due to things such as the relative lack of history for penny stocks.

However, and this is a big however, if you're comfortable with the idea that working with penny stocks is in a lot of ways a simple gamble, then perhaps you're ready to work on it. There are a few rules of thumb. First off, in order to mitigate the inherent risks of penny stock trading, you have to be *comfortable losing money*. If you aren't losing money, then you're in the wrong securities trading field. Most people who ever work with penny stocks end up losing more than they gain from them. Penny stocks, in a lot of ways, are very much like a casino slot machine: you put in your coin, you pull the lever, you watch it go around and around, and then you get a result. You may not like the result, but it's the result you got. And sometimes, you'll absolutely *love* the result. These are the times where you get triple 7s or a diagonal jackpot or something of the like. But regardless, it is your result. What's more is that there are a lot - a *lot* - more instances of somebody putting in a quarter for little reward than somebody winning the jackpot on a slot machine. The same thing carries over.

The whole fantasy story of the college kid who invested the money he saved in high school into penny stocks and became a millionaire by 23 is just that: a fantasy story. There's no legitimate reason for one to give this sort of thought any credence, and it's actually *dangerous* for somebody to boldly assume that they're going to be successful at all with penny stocks.

However, the biggest thing that you can do is monitor your spending. Penny stocks are a lot of fun, but just like the slot machines or the Powerball lottery, you (hopefully) wouldn't go in there trying to spend money that you don't have. You have other things to take care of. So if you're trying to invest *wisely*, something as speculative as penny stocks isn't the route to go. This is even more important and relevant if you're doing something like investing your retirement or 401k in order to get something like a 6% return on it.

There are safe securities trading situations, and there are unsafe securities trading situations. Working with penny stocks is very much the latter. It's generally common sense in the realm of securities trading that you need to have at least three different accounts: a savings account, where your money that you need for a later point is stored - this should *always* have money in it and almost *never* be touched, unless the purpose for which the account was started comes around; an investitures account, where you'll make "safe" investments with a long-term return, like bonds or treasury securities; and then your speculative fund, which is basically your gambling money. Your speculative fund can be dipped into for things such as penny stock trading, options trading, or anything where there is a high amount of speculation and uncertainty in the future of investments.

So if you've got money set aside, at least for a savings account and a few months worth of living expenditure, then and only then would I recommend going forward with penny stocks. If you wouldn't be willing to spend that money at the casino and go broke, then you shouldn't be willing to invest in penny stocks because the odds are good that the money will practically disappear.

Chapter 2: Picking the Right Broker

So you've made it this far. You've read through the pros and cons of penny stock trading and somehow managed to not be scared away by the fact that it's so risky. Perhaps you're even enthralled by the possibilities that come along with penny stock trading, or the inherent challenge - perfect! Well, before we get into how to pick the perfect stock in order to multiply your money and hopefully make you millions, there's one essential pit stop that we have to make: choosing the broker that we're going to go with.

The broker that you decide to use will actually have a lot of sway on the whole process of your trading. Your choice of broker can make a definite difference in how much you make. What's more is that you're going to want different brokers depending upon the exact situation that you're working with. For example, if you only have $500 dollars to invest, you don't want a broker with a $1000 account minimum, of course.

There are a few things specifically which you want to be mindful of when you're looking between various different online penny stock brokers.

The first are the surcharges. Different brokers will often add surcharges to stocks if they cost less than a certain amount of money. The charges aren't necessarily huge - usually something like a one cent surcharge for every share bought - but it still could add up, especially if you're trading in higher volumes.

Another thing is that a lot of brokers institute restrictions. These may pop up as either them restricting the *volume* that you trade, or the *manner in which you trade*. When they restrict the volume of your trades, they will often charge quite a bit extra on top for particularly large stock purchases. When they restrict the manner in which you trade, there are myriad ways in which they could do this. For example, some may require you to call them in order to place an order of a certain size, while others may say that you may only trade so many times per day. Neither of these are fun, but sadly, it's a reality of working with online brokers. Many online brokers won't have such stringent regulations in place, though, and you can rest assured that the regulations which *are* there are there for a reason.

So what broker do you go with? It depends on exactly what you need.

Overall

Many consider the two best penny stock brokers overall to be Charles Schwab and E-Trade. As an added perk to their other benefits, they both have a very strong customer support team and offer a ton of resources to educate you on how to choose stocks and play the market on your terms.

Charles Schwab is fantastic for a number of reasons. First off, they have a relatively low trade commission - only $4.95 for every trade you issue. The platform that they've established for trading penny stocks is top-notch and will absolutely not leave you wanting. The only downside of Charles Schwab is that they have an account minimum of $1,000, which may be a bit out of your grasp depending on whether you're wanting to get into this trade as a hobby or not. However, bear in mind that compared to some others (which we'll look at momentarily), this still isn't a bad account minimum at all. If you have the initial speculative investment capital to spend, then Charles Schwab is certainly a great option. As an added bonus, as of the time of writing, Charles Schwab will give you $500 cash to do as you like with if you deposit a certain amount of money into your account.

The other overall best is often considered to be E-Trade. Their trade commission is a little bit higher than Charles Schwab's, clocking in at $6.95 per trade, but it falls down to be equal to Charles Schwab's at $4.95 if you issue more than thirty trades every financial quarter. If you're intending to trade more heavily and more often, this may be the route for you. The fact that they benefit people who intend to trade frequently even extends into their current promotion: they will give you *sixty days* of trades without any commission at all if you deposit a certain amount of money. What does this mean for you? Well, it means that if you're a frequent trader then you could save hundreds of dollars on trade commissions. There are a lot of reasons that you would benefit from using E-Trade, but the low trade commissions combined with an easy-to-use and powerful platform alongside an amazing breadth of penny stocks to choose from and a Library of Alexandria's worth of important information for enterprising young traders.

Low Commissions

If you're looking specifically for brokers who will have a very light footprint on the amount you spend on commissions, then there are two more that you might consider. The ones with the lowest commission footprints are typically said to be Merrill Edge and Interactive Brokers.

Merrill Edge has a relatively high base commission at $6.95 per trade, but they don't have any sort of surcharges on top of that. That is to say that on top of the cost that you're paying for your shares, you pay

$6.95 and that's it. So where does Merrill Edge fall short? There aren't that many places, but one thing that you may find a tad out of reach is their $25,000 account minimum. Merrill Edge also certainly does not take any pains to cater to people who want to play the penny stock market. They allow people with lesser account values to trade on the normal exchanges, and also have a mandate that money placed in penny stocks shouldn't be more than 20% of their account minimum. Despite all of this, if low commissions are your game, then Merrill Edge just may be the option that you want to look into.

Interactive Brokers is the other one that has a very light commission footprint. They have no extra charges for penny stocks beyond a $1 minimum payment on every order that you place and a 0.5 cent per share commission. This is not much at all. You could trade 800 shares before it even really touched the base commission of other services, and that's not even including other services' surcharges and things of a similar nature. They also have a much lower account minimum than Merrill Edge, coming in at only $10,000. However, they do quite a bit to vet the people that trade on their platform, wanting to keep it mainly to professionals who have the money to spare. They have a monthly commission minimum of right around $10. They also require that you have a certain net worth and a certain amount of income depending upon your age.

Platforms

If you're looking for the absolute best platform - maybe you're a hopeful professional or someone who just really wants to spend a lot of time analyzing the decisions that they make - then there are two services that you'd really be hard pressed to do much better than: Ameritrade and TradeStation.

Ameritrade just may be one of the best platforms out there for a lot of reason. They certainly don't cater to penny stock traders, with a pretty high trade commission of $6.95, but aside from that, they're actually a great choice for multiple reasons. The first of which is that they have no account minimum. Granted, you may pay for this later in surcharges and commission, but if you don't have much to get started and just want to be a weekend trader with some of the extra money you've got lying around, then you and Ameritrade just might be best friends. On top of that, they'll give you a $600 bonus when you deposit a certain amount of money. But we're not here to talk about any of that, are we? Ameritrade isn't being listed for its low account minimum nor its hefty promotional bonus. Rather, it's being mentioned for its absolutely incredible trading platform. Ameritrade's *thinkorswim* platform is easily one of the best trading platforms out there, regardless of what you're trading. It's equally great for options trading, safer securities trading, and penny stock trading, for the sole reason that *thinkorswim* is absolutely loaded with professional-grade tools that will help you to do everything that you need to do and to know everything that you need to know. *thinkorswim* is one of the best platforms out there, bar none, and you'd be wise to try to work with Ameritrade in order to utilize it if a high-tech and limitless platform are among the things that you'd like to see in whatever broker that you go with. If you need something simpler for starting out, they also have a simpler web interface called *Trade Architect* which is far friendlier to newer investors.

TradeStation is the other broker worth mentioning for their platform. They have a trading platform that is immensely and endlessly complex. However, for the complexity, it is one of the most extensive and endlessly useful trading platforms on the market. More than that, it offers a plethora of tools and data which will help you to know that you're making the right buy every single time. Or, as much as you can know that while working with penny stocks, at least.

Ending notes

Those are the most worthwhile penny stock brokers to look into. They all have their own sets of features which make them the best in their own right, and all of them have their own set of pros and cons. I can't pin down the right one for you, simply because I'm *not* you. You, the person reading this book, could be any variety of things. You could be a college student with an extra $1000 from scholarships that you'd like to invest, or you could be a middle-aged man trying to make investments with some early pension money.

Again, I can't know your situation.

All that I can tell you is that every broker listed here is strong. Most of them have very strong educational tools that will help you to know exactly what you're doing even once you're finished with this book. Indeed, there's a lot of knowledge to be had about not only penny stock trading but trading in general, and a lot of it goes beyond what I can really cover in this book. That's why it's absolutely necessary that you take all the time that you can in order to learn all that you can. It's really easy to make mistakes, but by educating yourself, you can mitigate this.

Chapter 3: Picking the Right Penny Stock

I've already talked about how risky riding the penny stock tides can be. They're an endlessly speculative security and it's really difficult to know when you're making the right decisions. Things could go in any direction and at any time and the fact is that you simply don't know.

Add that on to the fact that the odds are very much against you as a trading layman. Think about it: the financial industry is big, and it has connections to every other industry out there. This means that every single day, there are people playing the market, buying and selling penny stock securities and making the best out of what judgment they have, and almost all of them know more than you. Why? Simply because they're more connected. As professional investors and financial experts, they have more insight into the companies, both from afar and up close. From afar, they can notice habits of successful companies and individuals that less knowledgeable investors will have absolutely no idea about. From up close, there are a huge number of investors and financial experts out there who are actually really close to these industries and who may have first-hand experience dealing with the companies in which they're investing, or they may have second-hand knowledge *about* the company from the friend of a friend of a higher-up.

So in short, yes, the odds are against you. Very much so, in fact. This doesn't mean that you *shouldn't* play the penny stock market. In case, it can be very wise and beneficial to do so, not to mention a lot of fun. But you need the proper background before you do so.

So what with all of that in mind, how do you make sure that *you* are picking the right stocks? You, with presumably little to no financial investing experience? Well, there are a lot of factors that can help you know exactly which penny stocks will win. I suppose that "exactly" is a bit of a hyperbole, actually, but regardless, there are trends that you can't miss when it comes to penny stocks.

Before you can understand that, you need to know more basic things about penny stocks.

Share price

The first thing that you need to know is that prices aren't always what they seem. The general line of logic is that penny stocks are far more cost effective. However, this isn't necessarily true and fails to take more factors into account.

This is one of the biggest things that people misunderstand about penny stocks. Just because they're cheaper doesn't mean that they're automatically worth more, or that you're getting more for less. Allow me to explain.

People who reduce the entire situation to this simple notion of "share price" don't realize the actual *value* of their shares. This is where the concept of *shares outstanding* comes into play.

For example, let's consider two companies, one of which has a share price of $0.05 and a market capitalization of $50,000,000. The other has a share price of $50 and a market cap of $50,000,000. They have identical market capitalizations, so are actually not faring too badly compared to one another in terms of investiture. Because the first company has a share price of $0.05 and a market cap of $50,000,000, we can surmise that they have 1,000,000,000 outstanding shares, with outstanding shares being defined as the number of shares which have currently been issued. This is different from "authorized shares", which is the number of shares that the company is allowed by the marketplace regulations to issue. Meanwhile, company B only has 1,000,000 shares issued. Thus, even though the two companies have a similar market cap and are faring similarly in that respect, the *shares* of company A has a lower price than the *shares* of company B, by virtue of the fact that there are more of them. Thus, the price of a company's shares aren't necessarily indicative of how well it's faring, especially not compared to another with a higher share price.

Side note: *market capitalization* has two meanings in the world of finance. The first is that of the sum total of the value of a corporation's stock, alongside its long-term debt and the earnings that it has retained. However, it can also refer to the number of outstanding shares multiplied by the share price to indicate how many have invested in the company and at what price. Here, of course, we're using the second, as we normally will throughout these discussions.

Dilution

This is the other thing that a new trader needs to be wary of when working with penny stocks - perhaps even more experienced traders won't have that much of an idea about how this concept works! *Dilution* refers to when the number of shares outstanding increases drastically and uncontrollably. There are a lot of reasons that this might happen. Among the most common are when companies decide to issue shares to others. This happens most often when they offer their employees stock options or when they start issuing shares as a mean to raise the amount of capital that they have. The second is actually extremely common among small companies as a means to raise the amount of money that they have, which is needed to operate and glide by until they have a meaningful occurrence (product launch, company milestone, new facility, and so forth). However, when this happens, it can dilute the percentage of the company which is owned by the investors who contributed *before* the company began to issue shares. This would cause the share price to decline massively in order to maintain a steady market cap.

When you're working with penny stocks, it's incredibly important to be sure that the company you're wanting to trade has a strong grip on the structure of its shares and the way that shares are supposed to be handled in different situations. If a company dilutes its shares constantly, the values of the shares will drop for the people who already *own* shares. In other words, you won't be making money, and that won't be a good thing. Be super careful about this. A company which dilutes often could make or break your penny stock portfolio.

How to Seek Out the Winners

This is what you're reading this book for, I'm sure. How to seek out penny stocks which will make you a lot of money in a short amount of time. Well, I can tell you that there's certainly no formula to it in any way, but there are a lot of things that you can do to increase the chances of picking a stock (or set of stocks) which will give you a noticeable return.

First off, you need to look at how a company works. Look at the bare essentials of the company and its actions in order to make a determination on whether it's a bright move or just a bold move for you to invest in them. For example, if they dilute their share prices often by issuing shares, do you really want to invest? Look at their structure, too. Is the company either drawing a profit, or will it eventually be able to gain a profit just by looking solely at the structure of the business and their current plans? Is it a realistic investiture? Could you see *yourself* using their product, if it came down to it? And more than that, is the company able to make a meaningful statement within its sector? By that, I mean will the company be able to compete at a decent level with its competitors and hopefully come out on top? Research its competitors, too, and see if it genuinely stands an honest chance against its competitors.

If you do this for every single stock which interests you, you almost certainly will be able to find a very promising company with a bright future ahead of it right then and there. It's actually incredible just how much context can do for you as an enterprising investor, so seek it out as much as you possibly can. Knowing the context of a company will help save you from making terrible and wasteful investments.

Yet another thing that you can do is to consider whether or not the company is in a sector where it's common or reasonable for a stock to be trading for less than a dollar. For example, the mining industry tends to have a lot of companies which trade for extremely low amounts, sometimes even just pennies. Because certain sectors rely quite a bit on the issuing of new shares in order to raise capital alongside hurting from increased competition within the sector, a potential investor must stay very alert as to the specific conditions in which the business they'd like to invest is residing. If the business suffers from poor conditions in a poor sector, then they likely are not a wise investment. If the business is in a sector with an extremely high level of competition then it's not terribly realistic to expect that some run-of-the-mill company will just start taking over the sector and succeed at the rate at which you'd like it to. Some, however, are *particularly* good within their sectors and have very strong plans. Such was the case of HudBay Minerals, who went from a small company with an even smaller micro-cop to a company worth two and a half billion dollars.

This may seem like obvious enough advice, but you'd be extremely surprised by how many investors and traders absolutely neglect looking into the basics of a company, like how much their shares are *actually* worth when you take into account shares outstanding, or things such as the company's basic structure.

Chapter 4: Trading Strategies

It's difficult to encapsulate penny stocks into a few "strategies". This isn't some 1990s video game where there's a set way to win a given level, and it's also not some 2017 video game where there are seven different ways to win a level. The hard truth is that there's no such *thing* as "winning a level" when it comes to penny stocks, because penny stock investing is simply just investing into a market. The market will go up and go down, and a win for one is a loss for another, somewhere. There is no market absolution. If you were to invest in the right thing, sure, maybe you could consider it a "win", but what if you sold and the stock continued to rise? Are you now a loser, since you didn't "win" as well as you could have? If a stock goes down one day, you might consider yourself a loser...

but what if it balloons in price the very next day? Are you a winner now?

The truth is that in many ways, playing the stock market isn't a game, no matter how fun it can be. And because it's not a game, there are no strict win conditions, nor is there even really a *way* to win, because there's no such thing as winning.

One can, however, do things which *appear* like winning. You can develop tendencies which will allow you to generally make the right decision, even if you don't ride a stock all the way to the top or even if things go awry and you have to watch it crash to the bottom. You can also develop a deep enough knowledge of not only investing but also the various industries in which you'd *like* to invest, such that you can make wiser investment *choices*. But to say there's a single investment strategy to win every time is silly, because it dilutes the multi-faceted and beautifully enthralling world of finance and trading into a simple dichotomy of winning and losing. It's not.

So with all of that in mind, I'm going to give you a lot of tips. I'd not like to call them "strategies", but you can call them that - they're strategies to help *yourself* and to help the *way you think*, so that you can look at the market in a better and more clever way.

So let's go through these one by one!

1) Examine the waves

The first tip is to *watch how the market moves*. A ton of studies on penny stocks and penny stock trading have shown that looking at the market with a short-term eye and trading in the short-term is far less risky than trying to trade in the long-term. This is understandable, too. Companies that tend to be based on the penny stock exchanges generally have one of two business models: they are either **a)** a new small business with a strong management team and a great product who just need some capital investment in order to get themselves off of the ground, or **b)** a low-profit small-scale operating company that isn't yielding too much of a result one way or another. By recognizing this and trying to trade in the *short-term* rather than the *long-term*, you can mitigate the risk - and there is a *lot* of risk! - that you accidentally invested in the latter rather than the former. Of course, this also should go hand in hand with doing a lot of research on a company and being certain that they're reputable enough and strong enough to be worth making an investment. But working in the short-term in combination with a fair amount of research can make a huge difference and make the risky game of penny stocks just a little bit less risky.

So how do you play in the short term? You play the day trading game of buying low and selling high. It's normal for stocks to be a bit like an ocean wave and fluctuate going from low to high and back. This is just the life cycle *of* a stock, and is not out of the ordinary at all. When it's in a low, you buy. When it's high, you sell. Rinse-repeat. If you do this with a company that you know well, you can make quite a bit of money.

2) Block out others

I don't mean to quit listening to your family or feeding your dog. Rather, new investors tend to be highly affected by malicious companies who opt to artificially make their stock more valuable than it actually is. This can be tragic for other investors, but great for the businesses in question. After they've gotten a bunch of new and inexperienced investors to invest in a stock for little to no reason other than word-of-mouth and the fact that they said the stock was a good investment, the owners of the company that spread the word about the stock will then sell their shares in order to make an easy profit.

This problem is becoming even more prevalent now that penny stocks have started to be more in the spotlight than they were before. Now, there is technology everywhere and constant communication between people. Penny stocks are no longer relegated to over-the-counter exchanges. Much like options, the fact that we've entered into an information age where people can spread their success stories has led to a lot of interest in penny stocks that wasn't there before. This is exacerbated greatly by the fact that penny stocks are very cheap, of course. This makes them rather appealing to people who aren't wealthy and would just like to weekend trade. These people normally play the penny stock exchanges like a lottery, putting their money where they think it should vaguely go and not thinking much more on it. They'll come back to it the following weekend and see just how well their investment went. These kind of gullible hopeful investors have created a perfect audience for greedy and malicious people out in the real world who think it would be perfectly hilarious to get unsuspecting people and con them into investing in a worthless company so that they could get a quick buck.

This sort of scam is called a *pump and dump*, and it's highly illegal. There are a number of different times in history where pump and dump scams have been all over the news and have been major silver bullets to the ever-fragile world economy. Perhaps the most well-known example of this scam is the Enron debacle.

Back in 2001, a company called Enron was one of America's largest electric and gas companies of all time. The executives at Enron decided that they would craft up a lofty scheme which would make them a ton of money, part of which involved a pump and dump. The scheme was so brilliantly devised that not even the most clever and experienced Wall Street financial analysts. The company was going under for various reasons, and was quite in debt. Through mark-to-market accounting, a form of accounting which aims to present balance sheets and company yields not as they actually are but as the investors and the stock market would like them to be, the debt was highly covered up. The Enron executives were reporting profits high enough in order to inflate the price of Enron's stock, and shortly before the company went bankrupt, nearly thirty Enron executives would sell the stock they had for over a billion dollars altogether.

They made a hefty profit, obviously. However, the resultant trial would end up landing most of them behind bars.

Another more fun example of this is Jonathan Lebed's pump and dump scheme. Then only 15, he was determined to prove how simply it was to use the internet in order to pull off a successful pump and dump scam. He bought many shares of penny stocks and then went on to promote them on message boards and chat rooms. He pointed at the price increase and told people to buy the stocks that he bought, saying that they were good investments. They were not. However, this wasn't known to the people who were falling victim to Lebed's scam! He would then sell his shares for a profit, leaving the stock rather worthless and with the other investors having lost a lot of money. It was at this point that the young Lebed landed in the eyes of the SEC. The SEC filed a suit against him. He would not end up going to jail and instead simply paid back some of his gains and made a promise not to manipulate the markets anymore. At the end of the day, he still walked away with hundreds of thousands of dollars - not half bad for a fifteen year old, if you ask me! The young Lebed was very clever, but what he did was highly and undoubtedly very illegal.

These are just two examples, and the first one shows that you don't necessarily have to be gullible to think that a stock is valuable when it isn't - pretty much the whole of the U.S. investing core thought that Enron was far more valuable than it really was.

However, if you keep your wits about you and pay close attention to everything that you're investing on, carefully going over the history of everything that you're wanting to work with, it's highly likely that you can avoid being a money-losing victim in the scheme of someone like Jonathon Lebed.

3) Don't expect too much

One of the reasons I'm sure you even picked up this book was because I bet that at some point you heard somebody say how much of an untapped gold mine penny stocks are. I'm sure that, at this point, you're a little disenchanted with that concept, especially after reading about all of the risk and scams that happen with penny stock trading. But maybe there's a part of you that's thinking "I can make a ton of money doing it, if I do it right!"

That part isn't wrong. In fact, it's technically right.

You *can* make a bunch of money pushing penny stocks, just like your son *can* make fifty dollars per day by opening a lemonade stand, or your dog *could* just relax on the couch when you get home from work instead of jumping on you excitedly. It *could* happen. That doesn't mean that it's likely to.

This goes back to the whole part about respecting the market and there not being "winners and losers". The best investors aren't the ones who make $500,000 off of a single trade. No, those are the *luckiest* investors. The lucky are always winners, but the winners aren't always lucky. You don't have to be *lucky* to be a good investor.

If you try to coast by simply on luck, let's say you *did* make $500,000 on a single trade. You decide "wow, that really well, I must be a masterful investor!" and invest $100,000 of the $500,000 you made in profit back into the penny stock market. You decide to invest in a stock which is rising, and it keeps rising, and you don't sell. Then it takes a nosedive. Maybe the owner of the company got caught in a terrible scandal or they had a major disaster at one of their main facilities. The stock that you bought is now worth *less* than you bought it for, and you've effectively lost a few thousand dollars. So what happened? Well, you didn't play it risky. Instead of setting a minimum and maximum amount that you'd be happy with, you got greedy and waited for a guarantee of gain that wasn't there. Instead of making back 125% to 150% of what you invested, you've now lost about 10%.

It's a bit of an extreme example, I know, but it happens on a micro-scale every *single* day. This is even more important in a market such as penny stock exchanges where everything is so volatile and moving from here to there and back again on a daily basis. If you go in expecting the world, you're going to be *intensely* disappointed, and probably will end up being one of the majority of penny stock investors who end up losing money in the process of investing.

Be happy with little bits here and there. Don't get greedy. If you get lucky, then fantastic! But don't rely on luck alone. Build up good trading habits *now* so that you have them when things do get a little bit rough.

4) Have a plan

This one is understated. It's always smart to have a plan no matter what you're doing. However, it's especially important to have a plan in something so volatile as penny stocks.

Now, it may be a little difficult to imagine having a plan when you're working with penny stocks. After all, everything is so all over the place all of the time. How can one possibly have a plan?

Well, the fact that it's so volatile *means* that it's important to have a plan. You always need to have a maximum that you'll be happy to gain, a maximum that you'll be happy to lose, and most importantly, an exit plan.

You need a maximum that you'll be happy to gain so that you don't sit down greedily on a stock when something is going your way. You could easily end up losing money this way - possibly more than you're really willing to lose.

You need a maximum that you'll be happy to lose because you don't want to sit around waiting for the stock coming through the tunnel when it may never do so. If a penny stock loses $0.13, of course it's hypothetically possible on a volatile market that it could make an utter swing and come out the other side and gain back its value really quickly, end the end making you profit. Of course it's *possible*. That doesn't mean that it's smart to wait around for this to happen, because it may not. And if it doesn't, then suddenly the negative $0.13 shares you're sitting on are negative $0.25 and you've lost a ton of money. Is that really something that you'd like to happen?

You need an exit plan because, well, you always need one. Have an idea of what you're going to do when the stock is within the boundaries that you've set, whether it's going in your favor or not. Are you going to sell it and sit on the money? Are you going to reinvest it? If so, do you need to be researching other penny stocks you may be interested in? This isn't as vital for securities as it is for futures, but it's still worthwhile to have an exit plan for your timing and your events afterward. Even one personally stagnant moment in the world of finance can make all the difference.

5) Don't let your emotions get in the way

This one is arguably the most important. You absolutely can't let your emotions get in the way. What do I mean by emotions? All of them. Greed, anger, sadness, vindication, happiness, whatever. When you're in front of your stock portfolio or your trading platform, all that you should allow yourself to think in are rational absolutes. Anything that isn't a rational absolute isn't worth your time and will only throw you off course.

What would be considered letting your emotions getting in the way? Let's say that you suffer a loss on a stock, and so to make up for that loss, you end up pouring even *more* money into the next investment that you make with the rationale that a profit on that will make up for both the losses and the disappointment of the prior failed trade. You decide to invest in another stock in a rush, only barely looking at the stock's history and the company itself.

Is that rational at all? No, of course not. But you'd be surprised how often it happens to people who'd like to be financial traders.

Money isn't an art, it's a science. Spare your emotions for art. Money is a game of math. The answers to your high school algebra assignments weren't allowed to change depending upon whether you felt happy, sad, or angry on any given day? Of course not. So why would you allow the way to handle your money to change with your emotions? The basic operations don't change, as they shouldn't. So why would anything else change? That's absurd. Money is money is money, and is absolutely; treat it absolutely, as you would math or chemistry.

So what can you do to avoid letting your

emotions get in the way? Well, having your money detached from the money you need to live can help, hence why earlier in the book I recommended that you only use speculative investing money that you can *spare* in order to invest in penny stocks. Using anything else is not only risky but a wholly bad idea. You need money to get by in life. Don't make the stupid mistake of mixing your gambling money with your light bill. That's how you lose your lights, and believe me, you don't want to lose your lights.

Don't forget to take time to decompress today and get away from your investments. Take time to meditate and possibly practice the tenets of Zen if you're so inclined. Take time to decompress - give yourself a massage to release your tension. Set up a very comfortable couch in front of a bright window and take time each day to sit in front of it and bask in the light, revitalizing yourself and calming your nerves that are surely on edge from a long day of trading and market unpredictability.

Do whatever you can in order to be certain that you *yourself* are healthy. You come first. When your body and mind are healthy and relaxed, your decision-making will follow.

6) Keep a journal

This is a big one. Keep a record of your trading patterns, both good and bad. Record your thoughts on each trade and what you're thinking about them, as well as how they go for you. If something stuck out to you about a company, record that. Do whatever you can in order to record your thought process when you're trading, as well as the results of that process.

Why do this? Well, there's hardly anybody better to learn from than yourself. I can guarantee that some of the greatest lessons you'll ever learn are from your own mistakes. And the mistakes of others, of course, but I digress. Learn what things go wrong for you, and try to keep up with your own head in terms of what you're thinking (or aren't thinking) when you make the good (or bad) decisions that you make.

You eventually will develop your own style of trading, and this will help you to find out what works for you. Maybe you find that you're actually rather good at seeking out companies which will be good in the long-term, and your strength is to invest more in the companies that you think will do well. On the other hand, maybe you'll find that when you invest a lot, you don't do as well. This would tell you that you need to make smaller investitures and probably diversify more. Everyone has a different temperament, as well as a different way of thinking about things. By studying your own thoughts and your own tendencies - how much you invest, when, the way in which you invest, whether you take profits or losses - will teach you a lot about the game of trading and about your own way of playing it.

You won't always make the right decisions. In fact, a lot of the time, you won't. That's where this journal will come in handy.

Chapter 5:

Start

Conclusion

Thank for making it through to the end of *Penny Stocks*, let's hope it was informative and able to provide you with all of the tools you need to achieve your goals whatever it may be.

The next step is to use the information in this book as you might in order to turn a profit.

As I said, penny stocks are very unpredictable. They're not a safe investment, they're incredibly speculative, and frankly, they're an all around bad idea if you're looking for a safe investment. Penny stocks are not in any way a safe investment. In fact, they're about as dangerous and volatile of a stock as you can find.

But, on the other hand, there are a lot of things that you can do in order to make them far safer to handle. I've covered a fair amount of that in this book.

I suppose that the last thing that you'd really want to do is get into some communities. There are quite a bit all over the web. The best place to discuss them is probably on /r/pennystocks over on reddit, at

www.reddit.com/r/pennystocks.

You can also keep up with Jet Life Penny Stocks and The Simple Dollar, at **www.jetlifepennystocks.com** and **www.thesimpledollar.com**, respectively. The first is a great place for you to get up-to-date alerts on the hottest penny stocks on the market. You can also sign up for email alerts which will allow you to get emails telling you what the best investments at any given moment are. The Simple Dollar, meanwhile, is a great place for you to learn all about personal finance and the caveats thereof. It's a great place to go in order to learn the very basics of personal finance, as well as all about the deeper topics which you may have questions about.

Last but not least is Investopedia, at:

www.investopedia.com.

When it comes to great resources for personal finance information, there are few that are of the same caliber as Investopedia. Most sites don't even come close. On Investopedia, you'll find a ton of information about all sorts of things regarding personal finance, penny stocks included. There will even be things that I didn't quite have time to cover in this book due to the time constraints.

In closing, penny stocks are interesting, to say the least. I know that over the course of this book, I've made them sound terrible. They definitely aren't! At least, not inherently. They have a lot of bright points, and a lot of people have made a lot of money on them. The people who lost money on penny stocks are, for the most part, impatient people who don't want to take the time to learn about what they're investing or people who simply lack the experience and knowledge to truly make the most of such a volatile market. It's extremely easy to simply not have the background or the know-how and not be able to effect any real change in terms of your financial portfolio, or perhaps even end up losing money. Hopefully, over the course of this book, I've taught you all of the essentials and essential tips and strategies well enough so that you can keep yourself on track and avoid falling in many of the traps that a lot of people who try working with penny stocks end up falling into.

So in closing, I genuinely hope that I've helped you in your journey of becoming a great penny stock trader. That's ultimately what I'm hoping for over the course of writing this book. Financial trading is a huge passion of mine, and it makes me happy to know that I'm helping people to get into something that I care so much about.

Penny stocks are a great and rewarding avenue for personal finance, and can also be a lot of fun, too. Don't put all of your eggs in one basket, know when to say "when", and you're on the right track to making a fortune, small or large, off of penny stocks.

Finally, if you found this book useful in anyway, a review on Amazon is always appreciated!